The YOU power in your marriage

Building a Better Union by Being the Best You

Ayo Ajiboye

Inspired Mind Resources

Copyright © 2023 by Ayo Ajiboye

All rights reserved.

No part of this publication may be reproduced, distributed, or transmitted in any form or by any means, including photocopying, recording, or other electronic or mechanical methods, without the prior written permission of the publisher, except in the case of brief quotations embodied in critical reviews and certain other noncommercial uses permitted by copyright law.

Table of Contents

Introduction: Understanding the Core Message of Matthew 7:3-5 1
    The Journey Ahead: Self-Improvement for Marital Bliss 2
Chapter 1: The Log in Your Eye - Recognizing Personal Flaws 4
    Self-Awareness: The First Step in Personal Growth 6
    Identifying Common Blind Spots 16
Chapter 2: The Mirror of Self-Reflection 23
    Tools for Honest Self-Assessment 23
    Embracing Vulnerability in Marriage 24
Chapter 3: Removing the Log - Strategies for Personal Change 28
    Practical Steps for Overcoming Personal Challenges 28
    Embracing Change for Marital Growth 29
Chapter 4: Nurturing Your Health - A Pillar of Marital Strength 36
    The Impact of Physical Health on Relationship Dynamics 37
    Practical Tips for Maintaining Physical and Mental Well-being . 38
Chapter 5: Cultivating Spiritual Growth 45
    How Individual Spirituality Enhances Marital Harmony 47
    The Power of Spirituality: 50
Chapter 6: Understanding the Speck - Empathy in Relationships 53
    Learning to See from Your Partner's Perspective 54
    Fostering Compassion and Understanding 55
Chapter 7: Communication as a Tool for Healing 58
    Enhancing Communication: Strengthening the 'YOU' in Your Marriage 58
    Understanding the Role of Communication 58
    Personalizing Your Communication Approach 60

    The Ripple Effect of Improved Communication 61

Chapter 8: The Dance of Intimacy 64

    Deepening Emotional Connection in Your Marriage 65

    Building Trust and Security 66

Chapter 9: Growing Together 72

    Shared Goals and Values... 72

    Aligning Dreams and Aspirations as a Couple 74

    The Power of Shared Experiences 74

    The Power of Building Memories Together............................... 75

    The Responsibility of Contribution 76

    The Role of Active Participation.. 77

Chapter 10: Maintaining the Balance - Individuality within Marriage 78

    Preserving Personal Identity in a Committed Relationship 80

    Supporting Each Other's Personal Growth 81

Chapter 11: Renewal and Reconciliation 85

    Forgiveness and Letting Go of Past Hurts................................... 87

    Rebuilding and Strengthening the Marital Bond 88

Chapter 12: A Vision for the Future 91

    Envisioning a Lifetime of Growth and Love 93

    Continuing the Journey of Self-Improvement and Marital Fulfillment 94

Conclusion: Reflecting on the Journey 96

    The Enduring Power of Self-Transformation in Marriage........... 97

Appendices:Exercises and Activities for Couples............................... 101

    Sade's Story: A Journey of Self-Discovery and Transformation.... 104

Introduction

Understanding the Core Message of Matthew 7:3-5

Matthew 7:3-5 NLT

3 "And why worry about a speck in your friend's eye[a] when you have a log in your own? **4** How can you think of saying to your friend,[b] 'Let me help you get rid of that speck in your eye,' when you can't see past the log in your own eye? **5** Hypocrite! First get rid of the log in your own eye; then you will see well enough to deal with the speck in your friend's eye.

In the journey of marriage, it's common to focus on what our partner could be doing better. Yet, as the scripture in Matthew 7:3-5 vividly illustrates, we often overlook our own bigger issues while zeroing in on their smaller ones. This analogy of trying to remove a speck from your partner's eye while having a log in your own eye is not just a biblical lesson; it's a practical guide for modern relationships.

This scripture, and the core idea of our book, "The YOU Power in Your Marriage: Building a Better Union by Being the Best You," converge on a powerful truth: ***the most significant improvements in our marriage begin with us.***

By looking inward and working on ourselves first, we set the foundation for resolving marital issues. Personal growth - whether it's spiritual, emotional, mental, or physical - plays a crucial role in the health of a marriage.

Every step we take towards self-improvement not only benefits us but also enhances our relationship. To improve your marriage, the best starting point is improving yourself. The health and strength of your marriage are inextricably linked to your own well-being.

A better you doesn't just contribute to a better marriage; it is the best gift you can give to your partnership.

In this book, we will delve deeper into this concept. We'll explore how embracing personal growth leads to a more fulfilling and harmonious marriage. Let's embark on this journey of self-discovery, understanding that in the quest to build a better union, the most transformative power lies within you.

The Journey Ahead: Self-Improvement for Marital Bliss

Imagine your marriage as a garden. Just like any garden, it needs regular care and attention to flourish. Now, think of self-improvement as the water and sunshine that nurture this garden. This is what our journey in "The YOU Power in Your Marriage" is all about - nurturing your marriage by nurturing yourself.

Why focus on self-improvement? **Because every small step we take to become better individuals adds up to big changes in our marriage.** It's like fixing a leaky faucet or painting a faded wall in your home; these small acts of care make the whole house more pleasant to live in.

Similarly, when we work on our own emotional, mental, and spiritual health, we bring a healthier, happier self to our marriage.

This doesn't mean we are at fault for all issues in the marriage, but it acknowledges that we have the power to make significant positive changes.

Throughout this book, we'll explore different ways to embark on this self-improvement journey. We'll talk about understanding and managing our emotions better, learning new communication skills, and finding ways to grow spiritually and mentally.

These aren't just tasks or chores; think of them as adventures that make you more you, and in turn, make your marriage more vibrant and fulfilling.

Remember, the journey to marital bliss isn't a sprint; it's more like a leisurely walk through that well-nurtured garden.

There will be sunny days and rainy days, but each step forward is a step towards a more loving, understanding, and supportive marriage.

As we embark on this journey, keep an open heart and an open mind. Be ready to discover new aspects of yourself and see how these discoveries can transform your relationship.

A better, more blissful marriage is not just about what you do together, but also about how you grow individually. So, let's start this exciting journey of self-improvement, knowing that every step we take brings us closer to the marital bliss we all seek.

Chapter 1

The Log in Your Eye
- Recognizing Personal Flaws

In this chapter, we're going to explore something really important: understanding yourself and how it can make a huge difference in your marriage. Think of it like walking through your house in the dark.

At first, you might bump into furniture or stumble, but as you turn on the lights, everything becomes clearer and easier to navigate. We're going to turn on the lights on how you see yourself and your relationship.

Let me share a story about my friend, Mike. He always thought his wife was too critical of him. But one day, when he really took a moment to think about his own actions, he realized he often ignored her suggestions or didn't take her concerns seriously. This was his moment of turning on the light. He saw his own behavior clearly for the first time.

This chapter does just that. It helps you see aspects of yourself that you might have missed before. These might be things that are causing issues in your marriage without you realizing it. It's about understanding your actions, your emotions, and how all of this impacts your loved one.

As you get a clearer view of yourself, you'll start to understand your marriage better. You'll see why certain things you do might upset your partner and find better ways to express what you feel. After Mike saw the light on his behavior, he and his wife started communicating better. Their arguments lessened, and they began to understand each other more deeply.

By the end of this chapter, you'll learn that changing and growing yourself can bring so much good to your marriage. Just like Mike, you'll see that understanding yourself is key to a healthy and happy relationship. Remember, it's a journey, but every step towards greater self-awareness is a step towards a brighter, more loving life with your partner.

Key points covered include:

1. **The Essence of Self-Awareness**: This section emphasizes the need for introspection in understanding our own behaviors, attitudes, and their impacts on our spouse. It encourages readers to ask themselves hard questions about their role in marital issues and to be open to feedback, highlighting that this process is not about self-blame but about gaining clarity.

2. **Identifying Common Blind Spots**: In this part of the chapter, it lists typical blind spots in relationships, such as not listening, being defensive, avoiding conflict, and taking our partner for granted. Each of these is explored with examples, showing how

they can lead to misunderstandings and strain in the relationship.

3. **The First Step in the Journey**: This section concludes by reiterating that recognizing and addressing our personal flaws is the first and most crucial step towards personal growth and improving our marriage. It's about turning on the light in a previously dark room, gaining new insights into our behavior and its effects on our partner.

Throughout the chapter, readers are encouraged to embrace this journey of self-discovery, understanding that recognizing their own flaws is not just about self-improvement, but also about nurturing a healthier, happier marriage.

Self-Awareness: The First Step in Personal Growth

Imagine you're walking around with a pair of sunglasses smeared with mud. Everything you see is unclear and distorted. This is what happens in your marriage when you lack self-awareness. You start viewing your marriage through a lens clouded by your own unacknowledged flaws and biases.

Self-awareness is akin to cleaning those muddy sunglasses. It involves taking a good, hard look at yourself - your attitudes, behaviors, and reactions - and understanding how they impact your spouse and your marriage. This process isn't about self-blame or guilt; it's about gaining clarity.

So, how do you start? Begin by asking yourself some challenging questions: 'How do I contribute to the problems in my marriage? What are my weaknesses?' It's crucial to listen - really listen - to what your partner, and sometimes others, tell you about yourself. It might feel uncomfortable, but it's an essential step for growth and improvement in your marriage.

> *You, like everyone, have blind spots - those areas in your character that are invisible to you but obvious to others.*

In your marriage, these blind spots can lead to misunderstandings and hurt feelings. Let's explore a few common ones:

1. Not Listening:

Have you ever found yourself so focused on getting your point across that you don't really hear what your partner is saying? This happens more often than you might think. It's a common issue in marriages, where truly listening to your partner can sometimes take a backseat. This occurs when you're so intent on expressing your views or defending your stance that you fail to tune into what your partner is trying to communicate. Remember, it's not just about the words they speak; it's about understanding the feelings, needs, and desires behind those words.

When we don't listen, several things can happen:

- **Misunderstanding and Misinterpretation**: We may respond to what we think our partner is saying, not to what they are saying. This can lead to misunderstandings and unnecessary conflicts.

- **Emotional Distance**: By not listening, we inadvertently send a message that our partner's thoughts and feelings are not important to us. This can create emotional distance and erode the sense of closeness and understanding in the relationship.

- **Frustration and Resentment**: Repeated experiences of not being heard can lead to feelings of frustration and resentment in our partner. They may feel undervalued and ignored, which can simmer and manifest in various negative ways in the relationship.

- **Missed Opportunities for Connection**: Listening is a fundamental way we connect with others. By not listening, we miss out on opportunities to deepen our understanding of and connection with our partner.

How to Improve Listening Skills:

- **Active Listening**: This involves fully concentrating on what is being said, rather than just passively 'hearing' the message. It includes giving nonverbal cues like nodding, maintaining eye contact, and verbal affirmations like "I see" or "I understand."

- **Empathetic Listening**: Try to understand the situation from your partner's perspective. Acknowledge their feelings and show empathy, which can be as simple as saying, "That sounds really challenging."

- **Avoiding Interruptions**: Resist the urge to interrupt or formulate your response while your partner is speaking. Give them space to express themselves fully before you respond.

- **Asking Clarifying Questions**: If you're not sure about what your partner is saying, ask for clarification. This shows that you are interested and engaged.

- **Reflecting and Summarizing**: After your partner finishes speaking, summarize what you've heard to confirm your understanding. This can also help clarify any misconceptions right away.

Improving listening skills is not just about hearing words; it's about understanding your partner's world. By becoming better listeners, we can transform our marriage into a more empathetic, understanding, and connected partnership.

2. Defensiveness:

Have you noticed how, when your partner brings up an issue, you might quickly become defensive instead of trying to understand their perspective? Think of defensiveness in marriage as a shield you instinctively grab to protect yourself. However, this often results in building a wall between you and your partner. This reaction typically happens when your partner raises a concern and, rather than seeking to understand their viewpoint, you instantly go on the defensive. This could be because you feel attacked, fear criticism, or don't want to admit fault. It's a natural response, but it can hinder genuine communication and understanding in your marriage.

Here's what happens when we become defensive:

- **Blocking Effective Communication**: Defensiveness shuts down the possibility of an open and honest conversation. It prevents us from understanding the real issue at hand and addressing it constructively.

- **Erosion of Trust**: Constant defensiveness can erode trust in a relationship. Our partner may feel that their feelings and concerns are not being taken seriously, leading them to withdraw or withhold communication in the future.

- **Escalation of Conflict**: Defensive reactions often provoke further conflict. A conversation that could have been a calm discussion turns into a heated argument, with both partners feeling misunderstood and aggrieved.

- **Missed Opportunities for Growth**: By being defensive, we miss out on opportunities to learn about ourselves and grow as individuals and as partners. Often, feedback from our partner, though it may be hard to hear, is valuable for our personal development.

Strategies to Overcome Defensiveness:

- **Pause and Reflect**: When you feel defensive, take a moment to pause. Ask yourself why you're feeling defensive and whether it's truly helping the situation.

- **Seek to Understand**: Try to understand where your partner is coming from. Listen to their concerns fully before responding.

- **Own Your Part**: If there is truth in what your partner is saying, acknowledge it. Owning up to our mistakes or shortcomings doesn't make us weak; it shows strength and willingness to improve.

- **Communicate Calmly**: Respond calmly and constructively. Use phrases like, "I understand your point of view," or "Let me think about what you've said," to keep the conversation productive.

- **Seek Feedback**: Sometimes, we're not aware of our defensiveness. Asking for feedback from our partner or a trusted friend can provide us with insights into our behavior.

Defensiveness is a natural reaction, but in marriage, it often does more harm than good. By recognizing and working through our defensive tendencies, we open the door to more meaningful and constructive communication, fostering a stronger, healthier relationship with our partner.

3. Avoiding Conflict:

Do you find yourself walking away from arguments, believing you're keeping the peace, when in reality, you're just avoiding dealing with the issues at hand? On the surface, it might seem like avoiding conflict is a peaceful approach to your marriage. It's akin to noticing a storm brewing and choosing to walk the other way, hoping it will simply pass. While this strategy might offer temporary relief, in the long run, it usually means you're avoiding important issues that really need your attention and resolution.

Let's explore what happens when we consistently avoid conflict:

- **Unresolved Issues Accumulate**: Think of unresolved issues as a pile of unopened letters. They don't disappear just because we ignore them; they keep piling up, and eventually, they become overwhelming.

- **Emotional Distance**: Continually avoiding conflict can create a gap between partners. It can lead to a situation where both feel they are walking on eggshells, unable to express their true feelings or concerns.

- **Miscommunication and Misunderstandings**: When we don't discuss our issues, misunderstandings can grow. What starts as a small issue can turn into a larger problem due to lack of clarity and communication.

- **Resentment Builds Up**: Over time, avoiding issues can lead to resentment. This can happen when one partner feels their concerns are never acknowledged or addressed.

- **Loss of Opportunity for Growth**: Every conflict, handled well, is an opportunity for growth in a relationship. It can strengthen understanding, empathy, and connection. By avoiding conflict, we miss out on these growth opportunities.

How to Approach Conflict Constructively:

- **Acknowledge the Issue**: Recognize that avoiding conflict is not the same as resolving it. It's important to face issues head-on, even if it feels uncomfortable.

- **Create a Safe Space for Dialogue**: Set aside a time and place where both you and your partner feel safe to express your thoughts and feelings.

- **Practice Active Listening**: Listen to understand, not just to respond. This helps in validating your partner's feelings and concerns.

- **Use 'I' Statements**: Express your feelings and thoughts using 'I' statements. This helps in communicating your perspective without sounding accusatory.

- **Seek Common Ground**: Look for solutions that address both partners' concerns. The goal is not to 'win' the argument but to find a resolution that strengthens the relationship.

- **Consider Professional Help**: Sometimes, it's beneficial to seek the help of a counselor or therapist, especially if avoiding conflict has become a deep-rooted pattern.

Avoiding conflict is a common response in relationships, but it's one that comes with its own set of problems. By learning to face and handle conflicts constructively, we can build a stronger, more open, and honest relationship with our partner.

4. Taking Things for Granted:

Have you ever caught yourself overlooking the small, thoughtful things your partner does for you or your marriage? In the daily rhythm of life, it's quite common to slip into a habit where you start taking things for granted. It's like strolling through a beautiful garden every day, but slowly, you stop noticing the beauty of each flower. Gradually, those small, meaningful gestures from your partner might not stand out to you as they once did.

When these acts of love and care start to go unnoticed, it can unintentionally diminish the appreciation you show for your partner's efforts. It's important to stay mindful of these small tokens of affection, as they are vital expressions of love in your marriage.

Here's how taking things for granted can impact your marriage:

5. **Diminished Appreciation**: The less you acknowledge the efforts of your partner, the less appreciated they might feel. This lack of appreciation can lead to them feeling undervalued or ignored in the marriage.

6. **Loss of Reciprocity**: Marriages thrive on a balance of give and take. If you start to take your partner's efforts for granted, they may become less motivated to maintain the same level of effort, leading to an imbalance in your marriage.

7. **Emotional Disconnect**: Not recognizing and appreciating the small things can create a distance between you and your partner. They might begin to feel disconnected or emotionally neglected within the marriage.

8. **Missed Opportunities for Connection**: Every kind gesture or effort from your partner is an opportunity for you to connect and strengthen your bond. By not acknowledging these, you miss out on deepening your marriage.

How You Can Counteract Taking Things for Granted:

- **Practice Mindfulness and Gratitude**: Make it a point to notice and appreciate the small things your partner does. Expressing gratitude, even for the simplest actions, can significantly enhance your marriage.

- **Regular Check-ins**: Dedicate time to regularly connect with your partner. Use this time to express appreciation for both the big and small things they do for the marriage.

- **Reciprocal Actions**: Respond to your partner's efforts with kindness and effort of your own. This creates a cycle of appreciation and care in your marriage.

- **Reflect on the Early Days**: Sometimes, reminiscing about the early days of your marriage, when every small gesture was exciting and appreciated, can help rekindle a sense of gratitude.

- **Communicate Openly**: If you feel you're being taken for granted or are taking your partner for granted, have an open and constructive conversation about it. Clear communication can foster greater understanding and appreciation from both sides.

> *Remember, in your marriage, it's often the little things that add up to a significant impact.*

By paying attention to and valuing these small acts of love and kindness, you actively contribute to the strength and joy of your marriage. Recognize the power in 'The YOU Power in Your Marriage'— understanding that your actions and attitudes, no matter how seemingly minor, play a vital role in nurturing and sustaining the bond with your partner.

Recognizing these blind spots is not easy, but it's essential. It's like turning on a light in a room you didn't know was dark. Suddenly, you see things you've been missing.

This chapter is the first step on your journey of self-improvement for marital bliss. It's about becoming aware of the 'log' in your eye - your personal flaws.

By recognizing and addressing these, you not only improve as individuals but also make a profound impact on the health and happiness of your marriage.

Let's bravely step into this light of self-awareness together, ready to see and grow for the betterment of your most cherished relationship.

Identifying Common Blind Spots

Have you ever had that heart-stopping moment while driving, where you almost missed seeing another vehicle because it was in your blind spot? That sudden realization that, despite checking mirrors, there was something you just didn't, see? Just like this happens on the road, it happens in your marriage too. In your relationship, there are blind spots – aspects of your behavior or understanding that you might not be aware of but are glaringly obvious to your partner.

> *These blind spots in your marriage could range from habitual behaviors to certain ways you communicate, or even the way you react to stress or conflict.*

Often, these are patterns you've unconsciously developed over time. They can be rooted in your past experiences, your upbringing, or even your fears and insecurities.

The tricky part about these blind spots is that they can create misunderstandings, hurt feelings, and even ongoing conflict without you even realizing it. For instance, you might think you're expressing your opinion clearly, but your partner feels you're being overly critical or dismissive. Or perhaps you believe you're showing enough affection, but your partner feels neglected.

> *Identifying these blind spots is crucial because it's the first step toward growth and improvement in your marriage.*

It's about becoming aware of the parts of yourself that you might not typically see – the parts that need a bit of adjustment or understanding. But how do you identify these blind spots when, by nature, they're difficult for you to see?

It starts with open communication and a willingness to receive feedback. It's about creating a safe space where your partner can express their feelings and observations without fear of judgment or backlash. This requires active listening, patience, and a lot of empathy. Sometimes, it also might involve seeking external help, like counseling, where a neutral third party can help illuminate these areas.

Remember, uncovering and understanding your blind spots is not about placing blame or feeling guilty; it's about taking steps to foster a deeper, more understanding, and connected marriage. As you begin to identify and work on these blind spots, you'll likely find that your relationship becomes stronger, more resilient, and more fulfilling.

Let's explore some common ones you might recognize:

1. **Assuming Instead of Asking**: Do you sometimes assume you know what your partner is thinking or feeling without asking them? This is a common blind spot. Making assumptions can lead to misunderstandings. Instead, try asking your partner directly about their thoughts or feelings.

2. **Not Recognizing Your Tone of Voice**: Your tone can sometimes convey more than your words. You might not realize that your tone comes across as harsh or dismissive, even when you don't intend it to be. Pay attention to not just what you say, but how you say it.

3. **Forgetting to Show Appreciation**: When was the last time you expressed genuine gratitude for something your partner did? It's easy to forget to acknowledge the small acts of kindness. Remember, a simple 'thank you' can go a long way.

4. **Overlooking Your Partner's Needs**: Sometimes, you might be so wrapped up in your own needs and stresses that you overlook your partner's needs. Try to be more attentive and consider what your partner might be going through as well.

5. **Jumping to Conclusions**: Do you often jump to conclusions during disagreements? This habit can prevent you from understanding your partner's perspective. Instead, take a moment to listen and understand where they're coming from.

Now, think about these points. Do any of them sound familiar? It's okay if they do. The first step to growth in your marriage is recognizing these blind spots. Once you're aware of them, you can start to work on them.

And remember, it's a journey, not a race. Each step you take towards understanding and addressing your blind spots is a step towards a stronger, more loving marriage.

The First Step in the Journey

Embarking on a journey of self-improvement in your marriage is both exciting and challenging. It's like standing at the base of a mountain, ready to climb to new heights in your relationship. The first step in this journey is crucial—it sets the direction and tone for everything that follows. So, what is this first step? It's the commitment to introspection and the willingness to embrace change.

Acknowledging the Need for Change: The first step is acknowledging that there are areas in yourself that need growth and improvement. It's like turning on a light in a previously dark room – suddenly, you can see what needs to be addressed. This might include habits, communication styles, or even deep-seated attitudes that have been impacting your marriage.

Commitment to Self-Improvement: Making a commitment to yourself and your partner to work on these areas is the next crucial step. This commitment is a promise – a promise to be open to learning, growing, and evolving for the betterment of your marriage. It's a vow to not just identify areas for improvement but to actively work on them.

Setting Realistic Goals: Begin with setting clear, achievable goals for yourself. These goals could range from improving the way you communicate in times of conflict to being more empathetic towards your partner's needs. Remember, these goals should be about self-improvement, not about changing your partner.

Seeking Support and Resources: You don't have to take this journey alone. Seeking support, whether from books, counselors, or even supportive friends and family, can provide guidance and encouragement. Resources like this book are here to help you navigate this path.

Embracing the Journey with Patience and Kindness: Remember, personal growth doesn't happen overnight. It requires patience, persistence, and a lot of kindness towards yourself. There will be setbacks and challenges, but each of them is an opportunity to learn and grow.

As you take this first step, imagine the possibilities that lie ahead.

> *A stronger, more fulfilling marriage is within reach. It all starts with that first decision to look inward and commit to being the best version of yourself. So take a deep breath, and let's begin this journey together, step by step, towards a more loving and resilient marriage*

Question to Ponder in Group Discussion

These questions are designed to encourage open discussion and personal reflection, fostering a deeper understanding and shared learning experience within the group.

Each member of the group should add their contribution or position on the following questions.

- What aspects of yourself do you think need improvement in the context of your marriage?
- How difficult do you find it to acknowledge these areas that need growth?
- What specific, achievable goals can you set for your personal growth in your marriage?
- How do you think these personal growth goals will impact your marriage?
- What obstacles do you foresee in your journey of self-improvement and how do you plan to address them?
- How important is the support of your partner, friends, or family in your journey of self-improvement?
- Can you share examples where support from others has helped you in your personal growth?
- How can you balance striving for self-improvement with being patient and kind to yourself?
- Why is self-compassion important in the process of self-improvement?
- How do you plan to track your progress towards your self-improvement goals?
- How will you handle setbacks or challenges that you encounter along the way?

- Can you share a personal experience where increased self-awareness led to a positive change in your relationship?

- What insights have you gained about yourself and your marriage through efforts at self-improvement?

Chapter 2

The Mirror of Self-Reflection

As you journey through your marriage, taking a moment to pause and look into the 'Mirror of Self-Reflection' can be transformative. This mirror isn't about your physical reflection; it's about seeing your inner self—your thoughts, emotions, and behaviors—and how they impact your relationship with your partner.

Tools for Honest Self-Assessment

Self-assessment is like standing in front of a mirror, but instead of reflecting your physical appearance, it reflects your inner self – your thoughts, feelings, behaviors, and how they affect your marriage.

This honest look at yourself is pivotal in understanding and improving your relationship with your partner.

Consider the following tools:

1. **Reflective Journaling**: Start by keeping a journal. This isn't just any diary; it's a tool for self-discovery. Write about your day, your interactions with your partner, and most importantly, how

you felt and reacted in different situations. Over time, patterns will emerge, helping you see areas for growth.

2. **Feedback from Your Partner**: One of the most direct tools for self-assessment is feedback from your partner. Approach these conversations with openness and the willingness to listen. Remember, the goal is to understand, not to defend.

3. **Personality Tests and Quizzes**: Sometimes structured tools like personality tests can offer insights. They aren't definitive answers but can be a starting point for deeper self-exploration and discussions with your partner.

4. **Mindfulness and Meditation**: Practicing mindfulness helps you become more aware of your thoughts and feelings. It's about being present in the moment and observing yourself without judgment.

5. **Professional Guidance**: Sometimes, it might be helpful to seek the guidance of a counselor or therapist, especially if you find certain patterns or issues challenging to navigate on your own.

Embracing Vulnerability in Marriage

Vulnerability in marriage is about letting your guard down, showing your true self to your partner, including your fears, hopes, and weaknesses. It's about being open and authentic, which can be scary but is vital for a deep and meaningful connection.

1. **Sharing Your Inner World**: Start by sharing your thoughts, feelings, and fears with your partner. It might feel

uncomfortable at first, but it creates a deeper level of trust and understanding.

2. **Asking for Help**: It's okay to admit that you need help or support. Showing this side can strengthen your bond as it allows your partner to be there for you.

3. **Accepting Imperfections**: Both you and your partner are imperfect. Embracing this fact allows for a more accepting and compassionate relationship.

4. **Building Emotional Intimacy**: Vulnerability leads to emotional intimacy. Share not just the good parts of your day but also the challenges and what worries you.

5. **Creating a Safe Space for Each Other**: Work together to create an environment where both of you feel safe to be vulnerable. This means practicing empathy, listening without judgment, and offering support and understanding.

In this chapter, the 'Mirror of Self-Reflection' serves as your guide to deeper self-awareness and vulnerability in your marriage. By using these tools for honest self-assessment and embracing vulnerability, you're not just working towards a better marriage, but also towards becoming a more self-aware, compassionate, and connected partner.

Group Discussion Points:

This discussion can happen between couples or groups of couples.

1. **Sharing Inner Thoughts and Feelings:**

- How comfortable do you feel sharing your deepest fears and dreams with your spouse?
- Scripture Reflection: James 5:16, "Therefore confess your sins to each other and pray for each other so that you may be healed. The prayer of a righteous person is powerful and effective."

2. **Asking for Help and Support:**
   - Discuss times when asking for help or support was difficult in your marriage. What made it challenging?
   - Scripture Reflection: Galatians 6:2, "Carry each other's burdens, and in this way you will fulfill the law of Christ."

3. **Handling Imperfections:**
   - Share how accepting your own and your partner's imperfections has impacted your marriage.
   - Scripture Reflection: Colossians 3:12-13, "Therefore, as God's chosen people, holy and dearly loved, clothe yourselves with compassion, kindness, humility, gentleness, and patience. Bear with each other and forgive one another if any of you has a grievance against someone. Forgive as the Lord forgave you."

4. **Building Emotional Intimacy:**
   - What practices help you build emotional intimacy with your spouse?
   - Scripture Reflection: 1 Peter 4:8, "Above all, love each other deeply, because love covers over a multitude of sins."

5. **Creating a Safe Space for Vulnerability:**
   - How can you create a safe and non-judgmental space for each other in your marriage?
   - Scripture Reflection: Ephesians 4:2-3, "Be completely humble and gentle; be patient, bearing with one another in love. Make every effort to keep the unity of the Spirit through the bond of peace."

Conclusion: Embracing vulnerability in marriage is a journey that requires courage, understanding, and a lot of love. It's about building a safe space where both partners can be their true selves. Reflect on these scriptures and discussion points to understand how you can foster deeper vulnerability and intimacy in your marriage.

Chapter 3

Removing the Log
- Strategies for Personal Change

Practical Steps for Overcoming Personal Challenges

In your marriage, you've probably faced moments where personal challenges affected the harmony between you and your partner. Think of these challenges as logs in your eye, as mentioned in Matthew 7:3-5. Removing these logs begins with recognizing and overcoming your personal challenges.

6. **Identify the Challenge**: Start by asking yourself, "What specific behaviors or attitudes are causing friction in my marriage?" Is it quickness to anger, lack of communication, or something else? Identifying the challenge is the first step to overcoming it.

7. **Set Small, Achievable Goals**: Once you know what you need to work on, set small goals. For instance, if you struggle with patience, aim to take a deep breath before responding in heated moments. Small steps lead to big changes.

8. **Seek Feedback and Act on It**: Talk to your partner. Ask them for feedback on your progress. Their perspective can be invaluable in guiding your growth. Remember, it's not about defending yourself but about understanding and acting on their feedback.

9. **Learn New Skills**: If your challenges are related to skills like communication or managing emotions, consider reading books, attending workshops, or even seeking counseling to develop these skills.

10. **Celebrate Progress**: Recognize and celebrate your progress, no matter how small. This will motivate you to keep going.

Embracing Change for Marital Growth

In your journey through marriage, as highlighted in 'The YOU Power in Your Marriage', remember that change is much more than just fixing what's wrong. It's about growing and evolving, not just individually, but also within the fabric of your marriage.

> *Think of change as an opportunity to blossom and to bring new vitality into your relationship.*

Imagine a garden where only the wilting flowers are tended to, while the rest of the garden is left untouched. Just fixing the immediate problems might make it look better for a while, but it doesn't help the garden reach its full potential.

Similarly, in your marriage, addressing only the visible issues is a start, but real growth comes from nurturing all aspects of yourself and your relationship.

This growth involves exploring new facets of your personality, learning new ways to communicate and connect with your partner, and embracing each phase of your life together with openness and adaptability. It's about looking in the mirror and seeing not just the flaws but also the immense possibilities for personal development and marital harmony.

As you embark on this journey of change, remember that each step you take in improving yourself contributes to a stronger, more resilient marriage. It's a journey of not just addressing the negatives but also amplifying the positives, allowing both you and your relationship to flourish in ways you might never have imagined.

> *That's the essence of 'The YOU Power in Your Marriage'— recognizing that your growth is integral to the growth of your marriage."*

How to embrace change for marital growth.

Embracing change in your marriage is like opening a door to new possibilities and a deeper connection with your partner. It's about recognizing that growth, both personal and as a couple, is a continuous journey, not a destination. This journey of change involves adapting, learning, and evolving together. It's about understanding that every challenge faced, and every adjustment made can strengthen the bond you share. In this journey, you'll discover that growing together isn't just about overcoming obstacles; it's about building a more fulfilling and resilient relationship that thrives on mutual support, understanding, and love.

1. **Understand the Impact of Change**: Realize how your personal change positively impacts your marriage. Improved communication, increased patience, or better understanding can lead to a deeper, more fulfilling relationship.

2. **Be Open to Learning**: View your journey of personal change as an ongoing learning process. Be open to new ideas, perspectives, and ways of doing things.

3. **Support Each Other's Growth**: Encourage your partner in their growth journey as well. Share insights, learn together, and be each other's cheerleader.

4. **Stay Committed**: Personal change takes time and effort. Stay committed to your goals, even when it gets tough. Remember, the rewards of a stronger, healthier marriage are worth it.

5. **Reflect on the Journey**: Regularly take time to reflect on how far you've come. This reflection will not only give you a sense of accomplishment but also show you areas that still need attention.

In this chapter, we've explored how removing the log in your eye – overcoming your personal challenges – is essential for your growth and the growth of your marriage. By taking these practical steps and embracing change, you are on your way to not just a better you, but also a better us.

The Story of Janet and Alex

Janet and Alex had been married for eight years. They seemed like a perfect match, but over time, their marriage had hit a rough patch. Janet was a dynamic marketing executive, always chasing deadlines, while Alex, a graphic designer, worked from home with a more relaxed pace. Initially, their differences had been complementary, but as years passed, these differences became sources of friction.

Janet often felt that Alex wasn't ambitious enough and lacked drive. On the other hand, Alex felt Janet was too absorbed in her work and didn't value his more laid-back approach to life. Arguments became a regular occurrence, and they slowly drifted apart.

The turning point came when Janet had to take a break from work due to health issues. During this period, she began to see things from a new perspective. She realized how her constant criticism had weighed on Alex, and how she had overlooked his contributions to their home and relationship. Meanwhile, Alex started to appreciate the pressure Janet was under at work. He realized that her drive was not just about career success but also about securing a future for both of them.

They decided to seek marriage counseling, where they learned the importance of embracing change. Janet started to appreciate Alex's creative spirit and his ability to find joy in the simpler aspects of life. Alex, understanding Janet's ambitious nature, found ways to support her career aspirations.

The most significant change came in their communication. They learned to express their needs and listen to each other without judgment. Janet embraced a more balanced life, appreciating the moments of calm Alex brought into her life. Alex, in turn, found ways to be more involved in Janet's career, sometimes collaborating on projects that needed his graphic design skills.

Through embracing change, Janet and Alex saved their marriage. They learned that change wasn't about losing themselves or compromising their values. Instead, it was about growing together, understanding each other's perspectives, and building a stronger, more loving relationship.

The Lesson: The story of Janet and Alex teaches us that embracing change in marriage isn't just about adapting to new circumstances; it's about being open to seeing your partner in a new light, appreciating their strengths, and learning to grow together. It's about understanding that change can be a powerful tool for strengthening love, respect, and connection in a marriage.

Intentional Change: The Key to Transforming Your Marriage:

The core message of the book, "The YOU Power in Your Marriage," centers on a profound truth: the transformation of your marriage begins with the transformation within yourself. Intentionally seeking to change and be the best version of yourself is not just a pathway to personal growth, but it's also a catalyst for rejuvenating and strengthening your marriage.

Why is personal transformation so crucial? Because marriage is a union of two individuals, each with their own thoughts, behaviors, and emotions.

When you commit to improving yourself — whether it's enhancing communication skills, managing emotions better, or being more empathetic — these changes directly impact the dynamics of your marriage. It's like repairing and polishing each brick of a shared building, making the entire structure stronger and more resilient.

This intentional change involves self-awareness, reflection, and a genuine desire to grow. It means acknowledging your weaknesses, celebrating your strengths, and being open to feedback. It's about understanding that change isn't a sign of weakness, but a sign of commitment to your marriage and to your partner.

When you transform, your marriage transforms with you. You bring new perspectives, a renewed spirit, and positive energy into your relationship. This not only helps in navigating through the existing challenges but also paves the way for a deeper, more meaningful connection with your partner.

The journey of personal change is continuous and ever evolving. Each step you take towards being a better version of yourself opens new possibilities for your marriage to thrive. It's about realizing that in the quest to see a transformation in your marriage, the first and most critical transformation has to happen within you.

In summary,

> *"The YOU Power in Your Marriage" underscores a vital concept: the health and happiness of your marriage are significantly influenced by your willingness to grow and change as an individual.*

Embracing this journey of self-transformation is not just an act of self-love but an act of profound love for your partner and your shared life.

Small group discussion:

- Discuss a time when a personal change or improvement you made positively affected your marriage. How did this change impact your relationship with your partner? Reflect on how your personal growth journey can continue to strengthen your marriage.

Chapter 4

Nurturing Your Health - A Pillar of Marital Strength

In "The YOU Power in Your Marriage," a key message is that your personal health is a fundamental pillar of your marital strength.

This chapter emphasizes that maintaining your physical and mental well-being is not just an act of self-care, but also a profound expression of love and commitment to your marriage. Your health serves as one of you best investment into the marriage and this is one of those investment within your control.

Physical Health and Its Impact: Your physical health directly influences your relationship dynamics. When you are physically healthy, you bring more energy, positivity, and resilience into your marriage. Regular exercise, a balanced diet, and adequate rest are not just personal benefits; they also contribute to a more harmonious and vibrant marital life.

Mental Well-being: Equally important is your mental health. Managing stress, being mindful of emotional needs, and seeking help when necessary are critical aspects of maintaining a healthy mind.

Remember, a healthy mind fosters patience, empathy, and understanding within your marriage.

The Shared Journey: Engaging in health goals with your partner can strengthen your bond. Whether it's a shared exercise routine, cooking healthy meals together, or supporting each other's mental health, these shared activities enhance intimacy and mutual support.

In essence, nurturing your health is a crucial aspect of nurturing your marriage.

> *By taking care of yourself physically and mentally, you are better equipped to build a stronger, more fulfilling partnership with your spouse.*

This commitment to personal health is a testament to the power of 'The YOU Power in Your Marriage,' highlighting how individual wellness is intertwined with the overall health and happiness of your marital relationship.

The Impact of Physical Health on Relationship Dynamics

Your physical health plays a crucial role in the dynamics of your marriage. Just as 1 Corinthians 6:19-20 reminds us, "Do you not know that your bodies are temples of the Holy Spirit...Therefore honor God with your bodies," taking care of your physical health is not just a personal responsibility; it's a way to honor your marriage.

When you're physically healthy, you're more energized, positive, and able to actively engage in your relationship. Poor health, on the other hand, can lead to stress, fatigue, and irritability, impacting not just you but also your partner. It can strain your marriage, creating a cycle of negativity and tension.

Consider how your physical well-being influences your interactions with your spouse.

Do you have more patience, more vitality, and a more positive outlook when you feel physically fit and healthy?

Reflect on how your physical health can be a testament to the love and care you have for yourself and your marriage. You must never forget the fact that the state of your vitality will have a direct impact to every area of your marriage.

Practical Tips for Maintaining Physical and Mental Well-being

1. **Regular Exercise**: Engaging in regular physical activity isn't just about keeping fit; it's about respecting your body. Even simple activities like walking or yoga can greatly impact your physical and mental health.

2. **Balanced Diet**: Nourishing your body with a balanced diet is crucial. Healthy eating habits not only improve your physical health but also your mood and energy levels.

3. **Adequate Rest**: Prioritize getting enough sleep. Lack of sleep can lead to a short temper and decreased patience, affecting your interactions with your partner.

4. **Stress Management**: Managing stress is vital. Practices like meditation, prayer, or even hobbies can help maintain mental and emotional balance. Remember Philippians 4:6-7, "Do not be anxious about anything, but in everything by prayer and supplication with thanksgiving let your requests be made known to God."

5. **Regular Health Check-Ups**: Keep up with regular health check-ups. Preventive healthcare is key to identifying and managing potential health issues early.

6. **Mental Health Awareness**: Be mindful of your mental health. If you're feeling overwhelmed, anxious, or depressed, seek professional help. Supporting each other in mental health is as important as supporting physical health.

7. **Shared Health Goals**: Consider setting health goals with your partner. This can be a bonding experience and a way to support each other's health journey.

Your physical and mental health are foundational to your marriage's strength. By taking care of yourself, you're not just ensuring your own well-being; you're also contributing to a healthier, happier marriage. This chapter aligns with the essence of 'The YOU Power in Your Marriage' - the understanding that personal well-being is intricately linked to the well-being of your marriage.

The Impact of Neglecting Personal Health and Hygiene on Marriage

When it comes to nurturing a healthy and fulfilling marriage, the importance of personal health and hygiene cannot be overstated. Neglecting these aspects can have far-reaching consequences, extending beyond individual well-being to the very heart of the marital relationship. Among the many facets of a relationship, one that can be significantly impacted is the couple's sex life, which is often a barometer of their overall intimacy and connection.

Case Study: Anna and Michael's Story

Anna and Michael's marriage started off strong, filled with love and mutual respect. However, over the years, Michael gradually began neglecting his personal health and hygiene. His lack of attention to his physical well-being, including poor dietary habits, lack of exercise, and disregard for personal cleanliness, started affecting their relationship.

Anna initially tried to approach the subject delicately, suggesting joint activities like going to the gym together or cooking healthy meals. But Michael brushed off these attempts, not realizing the impact of his actions on their marriage. As time went on, Anna found herself less physically attracted to Michael, leading to a decline in their sexual intimacy. T

his physical disconnects began to permeate other areas of their relationship, creating emotional distance.

Despite Anna's efforts to communicate her feelings and concerns, Michael's continued neglect made her feel unheard and unvalued. The lack of intimacy, both physical and emotional, created a rift that only widened with time.

Eventually, the couple found themselves in a loveless marriage, leading to its eventual dissolution.

Lessons Learned

From Anna and Michael's story, several critical lessons emerge:

1. **Personal Health is Integral to Marital Health**: Individual health and hygiene practices play a significant role in maintaining the physical and emotional bond in a marriage.

2. **Communication is Key**: It's crucial to communicate openly about issues, including those concerning physical health and attraction, in a respectful and non-judgmental manner.

3. **Mutual Respect and Effort**: Both partners must respect each other's needs and make concerted efforts to maintain their physical and emotional connection.

4. **Taking Concerns Seriously**: When a partner express concern about health and hygiene, it's vital to take it seriously as it reflects on their feelings and the health of the relationship.

5. **Preventive Measures**: Regular health check-ups, maintaining good hygiene, and leading a healthy lifestyle are not just personal responsibilities; they are acts of love towards your partner.

In conclusion, the case of Anna and Michael underscores the importance of maintaining personal health and hygiene, not just for one's own sake, but for the health and longevity of the marriage.

It highlights how the neglect of these aspects can lead to the deterioration of intimacy, ultimately jeopardizing the marriage itself.

Small Group Discussion:

Personal Health and Hygiene in Marriage

Introduction: This discussion revolves around the crucial role that personal health and hygiene play in maintaining a healthy and fulfilling marriage. We'll explore how neglect in these areas can impact marital intimacy and overall relationship dynamics.

Discussion Points:

1. **Personal Experience Sharing:**

    - Have you ever experienced a situation where personal health or hygiene impacted your relationship? How did you address it?

2. **Communication Challenges:**

    - Discuss the difficulties in communicating with a partner about health and hygiene concerns. How can these sensitive topics be approached respectfully and effectively?

3. **Health as an Act of Love:**

    - How do you view the maintenance of personal health and hygiene as an act of love and respect in a marriage?

4. **Balancing Sensitivity with Honesty:**
   - What are some ways to balance being sensitive to your partner's feelings while being honest about health and hygiene issues?

5. **Role of Lifestyle Choices:**
   - How do lifestyle choices (diet, exercise, etc.) play a role in your personal health and, by extension, your marital health?

6. **Supporting Each Other's Health Goals:**
   - Share ideas on how partners can support each other in achieving health and hygiene goals. What are some joint activities or practices that can be adopted?

7. **Learning from Case Studies:**
   - Reflect on the case study of Anna and Michael. What lessons can be learned from their experience, and how can they be applied in your own relationships?

Conclusion by the moderator:

Wrap up the discussion by emphasizing the importance of mutual respect, open communication, and joint efforts in maintaining health and hygiene in marriage. Encourage participants to take actionable steps towards incorporating these practices in their relationships.

Points to Ponder

- **Health Reflects Respect**: Your personal health and hygiene are not just about you; they reflect your respect and care for your partner and your marriage.

- **Communication is Crucial**: Open and respectful communication about health and hygiene issues is essential for maintaining intimacy and understanding in your relationship.

- **Small Changes, Big Impact**: Simple lifestyle changes, like a balanced diet and regular exercise, can significantly improve both your personal well-being and the health of your marriage.

- **Hygiene Matters**: Regular hygiene practices are key to physical and emotional closeness in a relationship.

- **Mutual Support is Key**: Supporting each other in maintaining good health and hygiene practices strengthens the bond and shows mutual care and respect.

- **Be Sensitive but Honest**: While discussing health and hygiene issues, balance sensitivity with honesty to ensure that your partner feels respected and understood.

- **Shared Responsibility**: Health and hygiene are a shared responsibility in a marriage, requiring effort and commitment from both partners.

- **Reflect on Impact**: Regularly reflect on how your personal health habits impact your relationship and make adjustments as needed for the betterment of your marriage.

Chapter 5

Cultivating Spiritual Growth

In 'The YOU Power in Your Marriage,' we delve into the profound realization that your spiritual journey isn't a journey you walk alone. It intertwines deeply with your marital life, influencing and enriching it in ways that might surprise you. Committing to building a Godly life will give you an opportunity to experience a Godly marriage.

This chapter is dedicated to guiding you through the process of deepening your spiritual connection, a journey that not only nurtures your soul but also brings a new depth to your relationship with your spouse.

Imagine your spiritual life as a river that flows through the landscape of your marriage. Sometimes it's a gentle stream, quietly nurturing everything it touches, and at other times, it's a powerful current, guiding and shaping the path ahead.

By deepening this spiritual connection, you and your partner can tap into a source of strength, comfort, and unity that is both personal and shared.

But how does your individual spirituality enhance marital harmony? It's like each of you bringing your unique colors to a shared canvas, creating a beautiful, harmonious picture.

When you grow spiritually, you bring into your marriage qualities like deeper understanding, patience, empathy, and a grounded sense of peace.

These qualities become the bedrock upon which a resilient, loving, and harmonious marriage is built.

Through this chapter, you will explore practical ways to cultivate your spiritual life, both individually and together with your partner.

We'll look at how engaging in shared spiritual practices can create special moments of connection and how respecting each other's individual spiritual paths can lead to mutual growth and admiration. We'll also delve into how spiritual conversations can not only deepen your understanding of each other's beliefs but also open doors to exploring life's big questions together.

Your spiritual journey is a powerful tool in creating a strong, loving, and enduring relationship.

As you read through this chapter, think of it as a map, guiding you to explore the spiritual landscape of your marriage. It's about discovering how your personal growth in spirituality can bring harmony, understanding, and an unshakeable bond to your marriage, reflecting the core essence of 'The YOU Power in Your Marriage.'

Deepening Your Spiritual Connection

Your spiritual life is a deeply personal aspect of who you are, yet it also plays a vital role in your marriage. Deepening this spiritual connection can bring a new layer of intimacy and understanding between you and your partner.

1. **Shared Spiritual Practices:** Engage in spiritual practices together. Whether it's prayer, meditation, or attending religious services, these shared experiences can strengthen your bond. Matthew 18:20 says, "For where two or three gather in my name, there am I with them."

2. **Respect Individual Spirituality:** While sharing spiritual practices, it's also important to respect and honor each other's individual spiritual journeys. Each person connects with their spirituality uniquely, and this diversity can enrich your relationship.

3. **Spiritual Conversations:** Openly discuss your spiritual beliefs, experiences, and aspirations with your partner. These conversations can lead to a deeper understanding of each other and your respective spiritual paths.

How Individual Spirituality Enhances Marital Harmony

Your personal spiritual growth can have a significant positive impact on your marriage. It's not just about religious beliefs, but about how these beliefs shape your character and interactions with your spouse.

1. **Moral and Ethical Values**: Your spiritual beliefs often inform your moral and ethical values. When these values are clear and

lived out, they can create a strong foundation of trust and respect in your marriage.

2. **Emotional and Spiritual Support**: Being spiritually grounded can enable you to provide emotional and spiritual support to your partner, especially in times of difficulty or uncertainty.

3. **Forgiveness and Understanding**: Many spiritual traditions emphasize forgiveness and understanding. Practicing these virtues in your marriage can lead to healing and a stronger, more resilient bond. Ephesians 4:32 encourages us, "Be kind and compassionate to one another, forgiving each other, just as in Christ God forgave you."

4. **Personal Growth and Self-Awareness**: Your spiritual journey often involves personal reflection and growth. As you evolve spiritually, you bring these insights and improvements into your marriage, enhancing the overall quality of your relationship.

In cultivating your spiritual growth, you're not only enriching your personal life but also bringing a depth of wisdom, compassion, and understanding to your marriage.

This chapter is a testament to the power of individual spirituality in creating a harmonious, loving, and enduring marital relationship, in line with the core message of 'The YOU Power in Your Marriage

Case Study:

In the heart of a bustling city lived Sarah and David, a couple who had been married for ten years. Their marriage, once filled with love and mutual understanding, had begun to show signs of strain due to the relentless pressures of modern life. David, a finance manager, often worked long hours, while Sarah, a schoolteacher, juggled her profession with raising their two young children. The daily grind left little room for communication, and soon, they found themselves drifting apart.

The Turning Point:

The turning point came during a particularly challenging phase when financial stress and family responsibilities peaked. Arguments became frequent, and the couple's once-strong bond seemed on the brink of collapse. It was during this tumultuous period that Sarah decided to reconnect with her spiritual roots, a part of her life that had taken a backseat amid the chaos of daily living.

Sarah started attending weekly bible study and practicing meditation and spiritual reflection sessions, seeking solace and guidance. As she delved deeper into her spiritual practice, she found a renewed sense of peace and perspective. It wasn't long before David noticed the positive changes in Sarah. Her calm demeanor amidst the storm of their challenges piqued his curiosity, and eventually, he too began to explore his spiritual side, joining her in bible study and meditation and attending fellowships.

Impact on Their Marriage:

This shared spiritual journey brought a profound transformation to their marriage. Sarah and David found a new way to connect, sharing insights and experiences from their new found connection to Christ teachings. Their conversations shifted from mundane frustrations to deeper, more meaningful discussions about life, values, and aspirations.

David's newfound spirituality helped him manage stress better and be more present at home, both emotionally and physically. Sarah's spiritual growth made her more patient and understanding, helping her to approach marital conflicts with empathy rather than frustration.

Rekindling Their Bond:

Their joint spiritual growth led to a rekindling of their bond. They learned to lean on each other, drawing strength from their shared spiritual beliefs. The challenges that once seemed insurmountable became manageable as they approached them with a united front, grounded in mutual respect and a deeper understanding of each other's needs and perspectives.

The Power of Spirituality:

Sarah and David's story is a testament to "The Power of Your Spirituality" in marriage. It highlights how individual and shared spiritual growth can be a beacon of hope and renewal in times of marital strife. Their journey underscores a key message of this chapter: that nurturing your spiritual life is not just a personal endeavor but a powerful tool to breathe life and resilience into your marriage.

Small Group Discussion: Cultivating Spiritual Growth in Marriage

Introduction: As we delve into the essence of 'The YOU Power in Your Marriage,' this discussion focuses on the vital role of spiritual growth in enriching and strengthening your marital relationship.

Discussion Points:

1. **Personal Spiritual Journeys:**
   - Share how your personal spiritual journey has evolved over time. How has this journey impacted your perspective on marriage?

2. **Spiritual Practices in Marriage:**
   - What spiritual practices do you engage in individually or as a couple? Discuss how these practices have influenced your relationship.

3. **Challenges and Spiritual Growth:**
   - Reflect on a time when spiritual growth helped you overcome a challenge in your marriage. How did your spirituality play a role in navigating this challenge?

4. **Balancing Individual and Shared Spirituality:**
   - How do you balance respecting your partner's individual spiritual journey with nurturing a shared spiritual connection?

5. Communicating About Spirituality:
- Discuss the ways you communicate with your partner about your spiritual beliefs and experiences. How does this communication deepen your connection?

6. Spirituality as a Source of Strength:
- In what ways has spirituality been a source of strength and resilience in your marriage?

7. Applying Lessons from Sarah and David's Story:
- Reflect on the case study "The Power of Your Spirituality." How can the lessons from Sarah and David's story be applied in your own marriage?

Conclusion: Wrap up the discussion by emphasizing the importance of continuous spiritual growth and its transformative impact on marriage. Encourage group members to explore and nurture their spiritual paths, both individually and as a couple, as a key element of building a strong, loving, and enduring marital relationship

Final Nugget to Remember:

"In your marital journey, remember that spiritual growth isn't just a solitary endeavor but a shared pilgrimage that can elevate the strength and depth of your relationship. Embracing and nurturing your spiritual life, both individually and together with your partner, offers a wellspring of understanding, compassion, and unity. It's through this spiritual connection that you can truly unlock 'The YOU Power in Your Marriage,' transforming not only your individual selves but also the very essence of your union."

Chapter 6

Understanding the Speck - Empathy in Relationships

In this chapter, "Understanding the Speck - Empathy in Relationships," delves into the transformative power of empathy in marriage. It emphasizes the role of empathy in fostering personal empowerment, a central theme of the book "The YOU Power in Your Marriage." The chapter is structured to guide you on a journey of self-discovery and growth through the lens of empathetic understanding within their relationships.

The chapter aligns seamlessly with the book's title, "The YOU Power in Your Marriage," by highlighting how empathy is not just about understanding others, but also a powerful tool for individual empowerment. It underscores that empathy in marriage is a two-way street that benefits both partners, leading to personal growth, stronger communication, and a more profound emotional connection.

Empathy, as discussed in this chapter, is presented as a vital component of 'YOU Power.' It's a skill that, when developed, enhances one's ability to navigate and enrich their marital relationship. The chapter positions empathy as an empowering force, enabling readers to transform their perspective and approach to challenges within their marriage, thereby fostering a healthier, more fulfilling marriage relationship.

Learning to See from Your Partner's Perspective

A Journey into Perspective-Taking

Imagine this: You and your partner are discussing weekend plans. You want a quiet evening at home, but your partner is keen on hosting a dinner party. There's a mild tension in the air. Here, we embark on a journey to understand what lies beneath these differing desires, discovering how perspective-taking can transform this typical scenario into a moment of connection and empathy.

Step 1: Walk a Mile in Their Shoes

Think back to a moment when you felt misunderstood by your partner. How did it feel? Now, flip the script. Consider a recent disagreement and try to view it solely from your partner's perspective. Was there stress at work that might have influenced their mood? This isn't about who's right or wrong; it's about understanding the 'why' behind their feelings.

Step 2: The Art of Listening

Tonight, as you sit down for dinner with your partner, practice active listening. Nod, maintain eye contact, and resist the urge to interrupt. After they've finished speaking, summarize what you've heard. This simple act shows that you value their perspective, and in turn, they are more likely to reciprocate.

Step 3: Embracing Their Reality

On your next date out, ask your partner about something they're passionate about. As they share, immerse yourself in their excitement or concerns. Try to feel what they feel. This exercise is about connecting with their emotional world, not just their words.

Fostering Compassion and Understanding

Picture a recent moment when your partner was upset or stressed. Did you feel an urge to fix the situation, or did you try to understand their feelings? Compassion starts with understanding and accepting emotions — both yours and your partner's.

Building Emotional Bridges

Next time your partner seems down, instead of offering solutions, say, "I'm here if you want to talk about it." This simple invitation opens a space for emotional sharing and shows that you're present and willing to connect on a deeper level.

Daily Acts of Kindness

Start a new morning ritual. Leave a loving note for your partner or make their favorite breakfast on a busy day. These small acts of kindness are powerful expressions of compassion and understanding. They say, "I see you, and I care about your happiness."

When Things Get Tough

During a disagreement, take a deep breath and remind yourself that this is an opportunity for growth. Approach the situation with a mindset of understanding rather than winning. Ask yourself, "What can I learn from this? How can we grow together?"

Reflection: A New Lens on Love

As you progress on this journey, take time each night to reflect. Think about the moments where you successfully employed empathy and compassion, and the times when it was challenging. This reflection isn't about judgment; it's about recognizing your growth in understanding your partner's world.

Conclusion: Embracing Empathy and Compassion

By practicing these steps, you're not just improving your relationship; you're also nurturing your growth. Empathy and compassion are ongoing practices that deepen our connections and enrich our lives. Remember, in the world of relationships, understanding your partner's perspective is the most profound expression of love.

Points to Ponder

- **Understanding Your Partner's Perspective:**
  - Reflect on a recent disagreement and try to see it from your partner's point of view.
  - Practice active listening without interrupting, showing that you value their perspective.

- **The Art of Empathetic Listening:**
  - Next time you converse, really listen, and summarize their points to show understanding.
  - Embrace your partner's emotions and passions as if they were your own.

- **Compassion in Daily Interactions:**

- Recognize moments when your partner needs emotional support, offering presence over solutions.
- Perform small acts of kindness regularly to show your care and understanding.

- **Growth Through Challenges:**
  - In conflicts, focus on understanding and learning together rather than winning.
  - Use disagreements as opportunities for personal and relationship growth.

- **Reflective Practice:**
  - End each day by reflecting on moments where you showed empathy and compassion, as well as challenging times.
  - Acknowledge your growth in understanding and connecting with your partner's world.

- **Empathy and Compassion as Relationship Cornerstones:**
  - Continuously practice empathy and compassion to deepen your connection and enrich your relationship.
  - Remember that understanding your partner's perspective is a profound expression of love and a pathway to personal growth.

Chapter 7

Communication as a Tool for Healing

Enhancing Communication: Strengthening the 'YOU' in Your Marriage

In your journey through 'The YOU Power in Your Marriage,' an essential realization is that building your communication skills is not just about enhancing personal abilities; it's fundamentally about nurturing the health and happiness of your marriage.

This chapter is dedicated to guiding you on how to strengthen your communication skills, a vital ingredient in the recipe of marital harmony.

Understanding the Role of Communication

Communication in marriage can be likened to the intricate threads that weave together to form the beautiful tapestry of your relationship. Each thread represents the various forms of communication between you and your partner - words spoken in love, understanding in silence, comfort in a glance, and strength in a gentle touch. This tapestry isn't just a collection of individual threads; it's a cohesive, vibrant representation of your shared journey, embodying the richness and depth of your connection.

> *When you communicate effectively, it's not merely the exchange of information. It's an act of connecting on a deeper level, where words and gestures transcend their literal meanings.*

It's about understanding the unspoken emotions behind a sigh, the love behind a smile, and the need behind a pause. This understanding becomes the foundation upon which trust is built. Trust, in turn, isn't just about believing that your partner will do as they say; it's about feeling secure in their love, knowing that they understand your needs, and trusting them with your vulnerabilities.

As you grow in your ability to communicate, you'll find that it deepens the intimacy between you. Intimacy here goes beyond physical closeness; it delves into emotional and spiritual realms. It's about feeling emotionally connected, understanding each other's dreams and fears, and sharing your innermost thoughts. This level of intimacy is what turns everyday interactions into meaningful conversations and simple moments into cherished memories.

Moreover, effective communication fortifies the bond you share, making it resilient enough to withstand life's trials. Just like a well-woven tapestry can endure wear and tear, a relationship grounded in good communication can withstand the pressures of everyday life. Whether it's the stress of work, the chaos of family life, or personal challenges, your ability to communicate can help navigate these challenges effectively. It's the assurance that you can face any issue together and emerge stronger.

In essence, every word spoken in kindness, every gesture made in love, and every effort made to understand each other, adds strength to this tapestry.

The beauty of your relationship's tapestry is reflected in its colors of empathy, patterns of trust, and textures of shared experiences. This tapestry, continually woven with the threads of effective communication, becomes a testament to the enduring strength and beauty of your marriage.

Personalizing Your Communication Approach

1. **Self-Awareness in Communication**: Begin by understanding your own communication style. Are you more of a listener or a talker? Do you express yourself best through words, actions, or emotions? Recognizing your style helps you understand how you contribute to the communication dynamics in your marriage.

2. **Active Listening**: Active listening involves fully concentrating on what your partner is saying, understanding their message, and responding thoughtfully. It's about hearing the words and also tuning into the emotions behind them.

3. **Clear and Compassionate Expression**: Learn to express your thoughts and feelings clearly and compassionately. Use 'I'

statements to articulate your feelings without placing blame, and always speak with respect and kindness.

4. **Non-Verbal Communication**: Remember, communication isn't just verbal. Your body language, facial expressions, and even your tone of voice convey volumes. Be mindful of these non-verbal cues both in what you express and in understanding your partner.

5. **Conflict Resolution Skills**: Use your communication skills to navigate and resolve conflicts. Approach disagreements with a mindset of finding solutions together, rather than winning arguments.

The Ripple Effect of Improved Communication

As you embark on the path of enhancing your communication skills within your marriage,' you'll begin to notice a significant and positive ripple effect that touches every aspect of your relationship. Improved communication is much more than the mere exchange of words; it's a transformative process that reshapes the way you connect, understand, and support each other.

1. Reduced Misunderstandings: One of the first changes you'll notice is a decrease in misunderstandings. Effective communication helps in clearly expressing thoughts and emotions, reducing the chances of misinterpretation. This clarity leads to fewer conflicts and a more harmonious living environment.

2. Deepened Empathy: As your communication skills grow, so does your ability to empathize with your partner. You'll find yourself better equipped to understand their perspectives and feelings, even if they differ from your own. This empathy strengthens the emotional bond between you, fostering a deeper sense of intimacy and trust.

3. Stronger Emotional Connection: Enhanced communication naturally leads to a stronger emotional connection. As you and your partner become more adept at expressing your feelings and listening to each other, you develop a deeper emotional understanding. This connection is the foundation of a resilient and loving marriage.

4. Transforming 'Me' and 'You' into 'Us': The journey of improving communication is about more than just enhancing individual skills; it's about changing the way you function as a couple. You'll start to see less of 'me' and 'you' and more of 'us.' This unity is not about losing individuality but about harmonizing your unique personalities into a stronger, unified partnership.

5. Continual Growth and Learning: Remember, mastering communication is a continuous journey. It requires patience, practice, and an open heart. There will be moments of triumph and times of challenge, but each step forward is an investment in the health and vitality of your marriage.

6. The Power of Effective Communication: As you progress on this journey, you'll discover that effective communication is one of the most powerful tools in your marital toolkit. It's the key to

unlocking deeper understanding, resolving conflicts, and building a lasting, loving partnership.

In summary, the journey to improve your communication skills is pivotal in realizing the full potential of 'The YOU Power in Your Marriage.' It's a path that leads to a more understanding, empathetic, and connected relationship, where both partners feel heard, valued, and loved.

Chapter 8

The Dance of Intimacy

In the intricate and beautiful dance of intimacy within your marriage, every step, every turn, and every shared rhythm profoundly matters. This chapter is an invitation to waltz through the delicate and rewarding process of deepening your emotional connection with your partner and building a robust foundation of trust and security. It's about understanding and appreciating the unique dance you and your partner share, a dance that is as dynamic as it is intimate.

Imagine each interaction with your partner as a step in this dance. The way you communicate, the tenderness of your touch, the understanding in your eyes – all these elements come together in a harmonious rhythm that defines the quality of your relationship. This dance of intimacy is not just about the physical closeness; it encompasses the emotional and spiritual closeness that you nurture over time. It's learning to move in sync, to understand each other's rhythms, and to create a melody that is uniquely yours.

The deepening of your emotional connection is akin to perfecting the movements in your dance. It involves not just hearing but truly listening to each other, sharing your deepest fears and highest hopes, and finding joy in the simple act of being together. This connection is built on moments of vulnerability, where you open up your hearts and allow yourselves to be seen and understood in your entirety. It's in these moments that you build a bond that goes beyond words, a bond that is felt in the heart and soul.

Trust and security form the foundation of this dance. They are the ground on which you stand and move together. Building this trust involves showing up for each other, being a pillar of strength in times of need, and being a source of comfort in moments of doubt. It's about creating a safe space where both of you feel valued, respected, and loved unconditionally. As you weave these threads of trust and security, you'll find that your dance becomes more fluid, more confident, and more beautiful.

In this chapter, you will explore how every step in the dance of intimacy is an opportunity to strengthen your bond and enrich your marriage. It's about moving beyond the 'you' and 'me' to create a harmonious 'us' that is resilient in the face of life's challenges and changes.

As you journey through this chapter, remember that the dance of intimacy is an ever evolving one, where each new step is an opportunity for growth, connection, and deeper love.

Deepening Emotional Connection in Your Marriage

1. **Sharing Vulnerabilities**: Just as a dance requires openness to your partner's lead, deepening your emotional connection involves sharing your vulnerabilities. It's about letting your guard down and showing your true self - fears, hopes, dreams,

and all. This sharing creates a space for genuine understanding and connection.

2. **Quality Time Together**: Like learning a dance, building intimacy requires time and dedication. Set aside regular, uninterrupted time to be with each other. Whether it's a date night, a quiet conversation over coffee, or simply doing activities you both enjoy, quality time strengthens your emotional bond.

3. **Expressing Affection and Appreciation**: Small gestures of love and appreciation are like the gentle steps in a dance, creating harmony and closeness. Regularly express your love through words, touch, and acts of kindness. Let your partner know how much you appreciate them, not just for what they do, but for who they are.

4. **Active and Empathetic Listening**: Truly listening to your partner, with empathy and without judgment, is akin to moving in sync with them in a dance. It shows that you value their thoughts and feelings and are fully present in the moment with them.

Building Trust and Security

1. **Consistency and Reliability**: Trust is built through consistent and reliable actions. Be someone your partner can count on, whether it's following through on promises or being there for them in times of need.

2. **Open and Honest Communication**: Just as a dance requires clear communication between partners, so does building trust.

Be open and honest in your communication, even when it's difficult. This honesty fosters a sense of security and trust.

3. **Respecting Boundaries**: Every dance has its rhythm and boundaries. Similarly, respecting each other's personal boundaries is crucial in building trust. Understand and honor the limits and needs your partner communicates.

4. **Navigating Challenges Together**: Facing and overcoming challenges together strengthens trust. Approach life's difficulties as a team, working together to find solutions and support each other.

In the dance of intimacy, every step you take towards deepening your emotional connection and building trust is a step towards a more fulfilling, resilient, and loving marriage. Remember, intimacy and trust are not static; they are dynamic aspects of your relationship that grow and evolve over time.

Embrace this dance with patience, understanding, and love, and experience the profound beauty of a deepened connection in your marriage.

This dance of intimacy is not just about the physical closeness; it encompasses the emotional and spiritual closeness that you nurture over time. It's learning to move in sync, to understand each other's rhythms, and to create a melody that is uniquely yours.

The deepening of your emotional connection is akin to perfecting the movements in your dance. It involves not just hearing but truly listening to each other, sharing your deepest fears and highest hopes, and finding joy in the simple act of being together. This connection is built on moments of vulnerability, where you open your hearts and allow yourselves to be seen and understood in your entirety. It's in these moments that you build a bond that goes beyond words, a bond that is felt in the heart and soul.

Trust and security form the foundation of this dance. They are the ground on which you stand and move together. Building this trust involves showing up for each other, being a pillar of strength in times of need, and being a source of comfort in moments of doubt.

> *It's about creating a safe space where both of you feel valued, respected, and loved unconditionally.*

As you weave these threads of trust and security, you'll find that your dance becomes more fluid, more confident, and more beautiful.

Here are key lessons to remember from this chapter "The Dance of Intimacy" in bullet points:

- Intimacy in marriage is a dynamic dance of emotional connection and understanding, evolving with each shared experience.

- Deepening emotional connection involves active listening, sharing vulnerabilities, and appreciating each other's presence, strengthening the bond beyond the surface level.

- Trust and security form the foundation of intimacy; they are nurtured through consistent, reliable actions, open communication, and mutual respect.

- Challenges and changes in life are opportunities to adapt and grow in the dance of intimacy, enhancing resilience and depth in the marital relationship.

- The dance of intimacy is not just about harmony; it's also about navigating conflicts with empathy, understanding each other's perspectives, and finding a shared path forward.

- Intimacy is about creating a unique rhythm with your partner, where both individuality and togetherness are celebrated and nurtured.

These points encapsulate the essence of building and maintaining a deep, trusting, and evolving intimate relationship within marriage.

Small Group Discussion: Navigating the Dance of Intimacy in Marriage

Let's delve into the heart of our marriages by exploring the 'dance of intimacy'. This chapter encourages us to look at how we connect emotionally, build trust, and navigate the complexities of our relationships.

Discussion Points:

1. **Sharing Vulnerabilities:**

- Share a time when opening up about your vulnerabilities led to a deeper emotional connection in your marriage. How did this experience change the way you communicate and connect with your partner?

2. **Quality Time and Connection:**
   - Discuss the activities or practices you and your partner engage in to spend quality time together. How have these moments contributed to the strengthening of your emotional bond?

3. **Building Trust Through Actions:**
   - Reflect on actions or behaviors that have helped build trust in your marriage. How do you maintain and nurture this trust, especially during challenging times?

4. **Overcoming Communication Missteps:**
   - Share an experience where a communication misstep occurred in your relationship. How did you and your partner work through it, and what did you learn from that experience?

5. **Adapting to Changes and Challenges:**
   - Discuss how you and your partner have adapted to significant changes or challenges in your life. What role did emotional support and understanding play in this adaptation?

6. **Empathy in Conflict Resolution:**

- Reflect on a conflict situation in your marriage and how empathy was used to resolve it. How did putting yourself in your partner's shoes help in finding a resolution?

7. **Creating a Unique Rhythm:**
    - Every couple has a unique rhythm in their dance of intimacy. Share how you and your partner have found and maintained your unique rhythm. What makes your way of connecting special?

Conclusion: Wrap up the discussion by reiterating the importance of nurturing the dance of intimacy in marriage. Emphasize the continuous effort required to deepen emotional connections and build a resilient, trusting relationship.

Encourage each group member to take away insights and apply them in their own marriages to strengthen their intimate bond.

Chapter 9

Growing Together

Shared Goals and Values

In the journey of marriage, the act of growing together forms a tapestry as unique and vibrant as your relationship. This beautiful tapestry, woven from the threads of your individual dreams and collective aspirations, becomes a testament to the strength and depth of your bond. In this chapter, we will look into the art of aligning your dreams and values with those of your spouse, creating a harmonious blend of personal ambitions and shared goals.

Imagine your marriage as a journey where each dream and aspiration you hold is a destination you wish to explore. Now think of your partner's dreams in the same light. This chapter is about mapping out a path that includes these destinations, finding ways to journey to them together, and celebrating each arrival as a couple. It's about understanding that while your individual dreams are like stars in the sky, shining bright and distinct, your shared aspirations are constellations that give meaning and direction to your journey together.

> *Aligning your dreams and values requires open, heartfelt conversations where you share not just your aspirations but also the values that underpin them.*

It's about finding common ground and building upon it, whether it's in your approach to finances, lifestyle choices, career ambitions, or family life. It's also about respecting and supporting each other's individual goals, recognizing that personal fulfillment contributes to the joy and satisfaction within your marriage.

The power of shared experiences in this journey is immeasurable. These are the moments that bind you together, that add color and texture to the tapestry of your relationship. Shared experiences, whether they are adventures in the great outdoors, quiet nights at home, or navigating the challenges of life side by side, are opportunities to deepen your understanding and connection. They are the stories you will tell in years to come, the memories that will bring smiles and laughter, and the experiences that will teach you about each other and about life.

As you explore this chapter, you'll learn how aligning your dreams and sharing experiences are not just pathways to a harmonious relationship but are essential elements in growing together as a couple. You'll see that in the dance of marriage, every step taken together strengthens the bond you share, and every shared dream achieved brings you closer. "The YOU Power in Your Marriage" is about embracing this journey together, weaving a tapestry of shared dreams and experiences that is as beautiful as it is enduring.

Aligning Dreams and Aspirations as a Couple

Your marriage is a partnership where both your dreams and your partner's dreams hold value. It's about finding a balance between these individual aspirations and weaving them into shared goals for the future.

1. **Discovering Each Other's Dreams**: Take the time to truly understand each other's hopes and aspirations. This might involve deep conversations about your passions, career goals, personal achievements, or even places you want to explore together.

2. **Creating Shared Goals**: Once you understand each other's dreams, start creating goals that you can pursue together. These could range from financial objectives, lifestyle changes, to joint ventures like starting a business or a family project.

3. **Respecting Individual Aspirations**: While shared goals are important, respecting each other's individual aspirations is equally vital. Support your partner in their personal goals and seek their support for yours. This mutual encouragement is a powerful way to grow together.

The Power of Shared Experiences

Shared experiences are the building blocks of a strong, enduring marriage. They are moments that you live, laugh, and sometimes even cry through together, strengthening your bond with every shared adventure.

1. **Creating Memories Together**: Whether it's traveling to new places, trying out a new hobby, or simply enjoying a quiet evening together, these experiences create lasting memories that become a part of your unique story as a couple.

2. **Learning and Growing Through Experiences**: Every shared experience is an opportunity to learn more about each other and to grow as a couple. You'll discover strengths you didn't know you had and overcome challenges that seemed daunting.

3. **Strengthening Connection and Understanding**: Through shared experiences, you build a deeper understanding of each other's perspectives and ways of thinking. This understanding fosters a stronger emotional connection and a sense of unity.

Remember that aligning your dreams and sharing experiences aren't just acts of love; they are investments in the fabric of your marriage.

As you journey through your marriage, remember that growing together means building a life that reflects both who you are as individuals and who you aspire to be as a couple.

It's about cherishing each step of this journey and recognizing that every shared dream and experience brings you closer together, creating a marriage that is as fulfilling as it is enduring.

The Power of Building Memories Together

Shared memories are the milestones of your journey as a couple. They are the moments of joy, laughter, and even tears that you have experienced together. These memories serve as reminders of the love you share and the challenges you've overcome. They are the stories you'll retell, each time reliving those moments and reinforcing the bond you share.

Every holiday spent together, every anniversary celebrated, and even the small, seemingly mundane moments like cooking dinner together or enjoying a quiet evening walk, contribute to this rich collection of memories. They are the threads that connect your past with your present, shaping your future.

These experiences become a source of strength and comfort, especially during times of difficulty, serving as a reminder of the happiness and love that you have cultivated together.

The Responsibility of Contribution

In the creation of these memories, it is essential for both partners to be active contributors. This means taking the initiative to plan and engage in activities that both of you enjoy. It's about being present, not just physically, but emotionally and mentally as well. When both partners contribute, it ensures that the experiences you are creating are meaningful and fulfilling for both of you.

Every individual brings their own interests, passions, and perspectives to a relationship. When these are shared, they add depth and diversity to the experiences you create together. It's important to be open to trying new things that your partner enjoys and to share your own interests with them.

This mutual exchange enriches your relationship, allowing you both to grow and learn together.

The Role of Active Participation

Active participation in building memories means being fully engaged in the experience. It's about putting aside distractions, whether they be from work, technology, or other external pressures, and focusing on the moment you are sharing with your partner. It's in these moments of undivided attention that the most meaningful interactions occur, and the most cherished memories are made.

In conclusion, the act of building memories together is a powerful tool in the dance of marriage. It requires both partners to actively participate and contribute, creating experiences that are not just shared but deeply valued.

These memories become the foundation upon which your marriage grows stronger and more vibrant over time. They are the legacy of love that you build together, a testament to the enduring power of shared experiences in your marital journey.

Chapter 10

Maintaining the Balance - Individuality within Marriage

Marriage, often envisioned as a harmonious dance between two souls, finds its true beauty in the unique individuality each partner brings to the floor. This chapter delves into the intricate art of maintaining your personal identity while being deeply intertwined in a committed relationship. It's a dance of balance, where preserving your essence is as crucial as nurturing the bond you share with your partner.

The journey of marriage is not about losing yourself in the union but rather about bringing your true self into it. Your individuality – your interests, passions, and beliefs – is like a palette of colors that you bring to the canvas of your marriage. It's these colors that add depth, texture, and vibrancy to the picture of your life together.

> *Embracing your personal interests and continuing to pursue the activities that resonate with your soul are not acts of selfishness; they are expressions of your unique*

These pursuits are essential, allowing you to remain connected to your essence and bring a sense of fulfillment and joy into your relationship.

Equally important in this dance of marriage is the space and time you give to yourself and to each other. Personal space is a sanctuary where you can reconnect with your inner self, indulge in your interests, and just be.

Time spent apart, engaging in individual activities or with friends, is not a gap in your togetherness but a breath of fresh air that rejuvenates your relationship.

It allows you to return to your partner enriched with experiences and stories to share, adding new layers to your shared life.

> *In this delicate balance, your voice – your opinions, beliefs, and perspectives – plays a pivotal role.*

Communicating your views adds richness to your conversations and decision-making processes, ensuring that the relationship is a true partnership.

Supporting each other's personal growth is an act of love and respect. It's about being the cheerleader for your spouse's dreams and aspirations, celebrating their successes, and offering support through their challenges.

This support is a powerful force that propels both of you forward, not just as a couple but as individuals.

Your partner's growth adds to your own, and together, you build a relationship that is dynamic, evolving, and deeply fulfilling.

It's about understanding that the health and vitality of your relationship depend on the balance between celebrating your togetherness and honoring your personal identities. is a testament to the fact that in a marriage, growing together involves growing as individuals – a dance where each step of personal growth is a step towards a richer, more loving union.

Preserving Personal Identity in a Committed Relationship

Your identity is like a fingerprint – unique, intrinsic, and defining. In the journey of marriage, it's crucial that this identity is not lost but celebrated and respected. Preserving your personal identity means staying true to who you are – your interests, passions, beliefs, and aspirations. It's about continuing to nurture the qualities and hobbies that make you, you.

1. **Embracing Your Interests**: Continue to engage in activities that you love. Whether it's a sport, an art form, or a hobby, these activities are vital for your self-expression and happiness. They're a reminder that while you are part of a 'we,' you are also an 'I.'

2. **Personal Space and Time**: Understand the importance of personal space and time. It's healthy to spend time apart, engaging in individual activities. This time apart can rejuvenate you and bring fresh energy to your marriage.

3. **Voice Your Opinions and Beliefs**: In a marriage, your views and beliefs should be heard and respected. Communicating your perspectives contributes to a richer, more diverse understanding between you and your partner.

Supporting Each Other's Personal Growth

A marriage thrives when both partners grow not just together but also as individuals. Supporting each other's personal growth is about encouraging each other to pursue goals, dreams, and personal development.

1. **Encourage Each Other's Goals**: Be your partner's cheerleader. Encourage them to pursue their goals and dreams and offer support in whatever way they need.

2. **Celebrate Individual Achievements**: Take joy in your partner's successes and let them share in yours. Celebrating these achievements reinforces the value of each person's individual journey within the marriage.

3. **Learn from Each Other**: Your partner's unique experiences and perspectives are a treasure trove of learning. Be open to learning from each other. This not only fosters personal growth but also deepens your mutual understanding and respect.

In maintaining the balance of individuality within marriage, you're not just preserving your essence; you're enriching the fabric of your relationship.

> *This chapter guides you in honoring and supporting each other's individuality, understanding that it is in the celebration of both your uniqueness and your togetherness that your marriage flourishes.*

"The YOU Power in Your Marriage" is about recognizing that a healthy marriage thrives on the balance of shared love and individual identity, where each partner is free to grow, express, and be their true self.

Small Group Discussion: Nurturing Individuality within Marriage

Discussion Points:

1. **Sharing Personal Interests:**
   - Share an interest or hobby you pursue outside of your marriage. How does this activity contribute to your sense of self and personal happiness?
   - Discuss how your partner supports your individual interests and how you support theirs.

2. **Importance of Personal Space:**
   - Reflect on how personal space and time alone contribute to the health of your marriage. Share how you and your partner manage to give each other this space.

3. **Balancing Togetherness and Individuality:**
   - Discuss the challenges and rewards of balancing your individual identity with the shared identity as a couple. How do you maintain this balance in your relationship?

4. **Communication of Personal Needs and Boundaries:**
   - Talk about how you communicate your need for individuality to your partner. Share strategies that have worked in respecting each other's boundaries while maintaining closeness.

5. **Celebrating Each Other's Growth and Achievements:**
   - Share a moment when celebrating your partner's personal achievement brought joy and strength to your marriage.

Discuss the importance of acknowledging and celebrating these individual successes.

6. **Learning from Each Other:**
   - Reflect on what you have learned from your partner's individual pursuits and interests. How has this contributed to the growth and enrichment of your relationship?

Conclusion: Conclude the discussion by emphasizing the significance of nurturing individuality for a healthy and vibrant marriage. Encourage each member to continue supporting their partner's personal growth and to cherish the unique contributions that each person brings to their relationship.

Chapter 11

Renewal and Reconciliation

In the journey of marriage, akin to the journey of life, there are inevitable moments of stumbling. These are the times when misunderstandings cloud our communication, when disagreements turn into conflicts, and when past hurts linger like shadows over our present. This chapter delves into the healing realms of forgiveness and reconciliation.

It's about understanding the transformative power of forgiveness, mastering the art of letting go of past hurts, and navigating the path towards healing and strengthening the bond you share with your partner.

Forgiveness in a marriage is a powerful act of love and strength. It's about opening your heart to let go of the bitterness and pain that past mistakes, whether yours or your partner's, have sown.

> *This process of forgiveness is not about forgetting or excusing the wrongs but rather about liberating yourself from the weight of resentment.*

It's a choice to no longer let past grievances define your relationship's future.

The act of forgiving, be it forgiving your partner or yourself, paves the way for emotional healing and renewal. It creates a space where understanding can blossom and where the seeds of trust can be replanted.

Letting go of past hurts is a crucial step in this journey. It involves acknowledging the pain, understanding its impact on your relationship, and then consciously deciding to move forward.

This step is often challenging, as it requires not only immense emotional strength but also a deep sense of empathy and compassion.

By empathizing with your partner and understanding their perspective, you pave the way for mutual healing and reconnection.

The journey towards rebuilding and strengthening your marital bond is like reconstructing a bridge that has been weathered by time and storms. It requires both patience and perseverance.

Rebuilding trust is a gradual process that is nurtured through consistent, trustworthy actions. It's about showing up for each other, being reliable, and demonstrating through actions and words that you are both committed to the health and future of your marriage.

Reconnecting with your partner involves rediscovering the joy and love that brought you together.

It might mean revisiting old memories, creating new ones, or simply finding joy in the everyday moments you share. It's about reigniting the spark that kindled your love and allowing it to grow into a steady, warm flame.

Lastly, creating a shared vision for the future is an essential step in strengthening your marriage. This vision, co-created by you and your partner, should encompass both your individual aspirations and your collective goals. It serves as a compass, guiding you both on a path that leads to a future where you grow not just as individuals, but also as a couple.

Forgiveness and Letting Go of Past Hurts

Forgiveness in marriage is like opening a window to let in fresh air after a storm. It's about releasing the grip of past grievances to make room for peace and understanding. This process starts with acknowledging the pain, both your own and your partner's. Recognizing that holding onto resentment harms not just your partner but also you is a crucial realization.

1. **Understanding Forgiveness**: Forgiveness isn't about forgetting or excusing hurtful actions; it's about choosing to release resentment. It's a decision to not let past hurts dictate the future of your relationship.

2. **The Path to Forgiveness**: Begin with empathy. Try to understand the situation from your partner's perspective. Communicate openly about your feelings and listen to theirs. This mutual understanding lays the groundwork for genuine forgiveness.

3. **Self-Forgiveness**: Sometimes, you also need to forgive yourself. Reflect on your actions and their impacts, learn from them, and then let go of self-blame. Self-forgiveness is essential for your emotional well-being and for moving forward in your relationship.

Rebuilding and Strengthening the Marital Bond

Once the process of forgiveness starts, the next steps are about rebuilding trust and reinforcing the bond you share. Rebuilding isn't a quick fix; it's a journey of reconnection and rediscovery.

1. **Re-establishing Trust**: Trust is rebuilt through consistent, trustworthy actions over time. Be reliable, keep promises, and show through your actions that you are committed to the health of your marriage.

2. **Renewing Your Connection**: Find ways to reconnect with your partner. This could be through shared activities, date nights, or simply spending quality time together. It's about rekindling the love and affection that brought you together in the first place.

3. **Creating a Shared Vision for the Future**: Work together to create a vision for your future. This shared vision should include both your individual goals and your aspirations as a couple. It's a roadmap that guides your relationship towards a shared destination.

In this chapter, you'll learn that renewal and reconciliation are not just about overcoming challenges; they're about growing stronger and more connected through them.

> *"The YOU Power in Your Marriage" is about understanding that every obstacle is an opportunity for growth, every act of forgiveness is a step towards peace, and every effort to rebuild is a testament to the resilience and commitment in your marriage.*

Summary of Chapter 11:

The Journey of Forgiveness: Emphasizes the transformative power of forgiveness in marriage, highlighting it as an act of love and strength that involves letting go of bitterness and resentment from past mistakes.

- **Art of Letting Go**: Focuses on the importance of releasing past hurts to move forward in the relationship. It involves acknowledging the pain, understanding its impact, and choosing to heal and progress.

- **Rebuilding Trust**: Discusses the gradual process of rebuilding trust through consistent, reliable actions, and open communication. It's about re-establishing the foundation of trust eroded by past conflicts or misunderstandings.

- **Reconnecting with Your Partner**: Encourages rediscovering the joy and love in the relationship, which includes creating new memories and finding joy in everyday moments together.

- **Creating a Shared Future Vision**: Highlights the importance of developing a mutual vision for the future that includes both individual aspirations and collective goals, guiding the relationship towards growth and fulfillment.

- **Navigating Challenges as Opportunities**: Frames challenges and conflicts as opportunities for deeper understanding and growth, turning past hurts into lesson of love and resilience.

- **Strength, Commitment, and Love**: Reinforces that every step towards forgiveness and rebuilding is a testament to the strength, commitment, and love in the marriage.

This summary encapsulates the key themes and messages of Chapter 11, focusing on the processes of healing, forgiveness, and strengthening the marital bond.

Chapter 12

A Vision for the Future

In the grand journey of marriage, creating a vision for the future is akin to setting the sails on an expansive voyage, one that guides you and your partner towards a horizon brimming with opportunities for growth, love, and fulfillment. This is an invitation to you and your spouse to envision a future together that transcends mere survival through the years.

It's about crafting a journey that's characterized by thriving in unison, growing both as individuals and as a couple, and discovering deep joy and satisfaction in the intricacies of your shared life.

Envisioning a lifetime together involves much more than foreseeing a series of events or milestones. It's about imagining the quality of life you wish to share. Think of this vision as a canvas on which you and your partner paint your dreams, hopes, and aspirations. It's a canvas filled with the colors of shared experiences, the textures of mutual support, and the hues of personal passions. This vision is not static; it evolves and grows as you do, adapting to the changes and challenges that life inevitably brings.

Creating this vision means sitting down together and openly discussing what each of you desires for the future. It's about aligning your dreams and aspirations, not just in the grand scheme of things like career ambitions or retirement plans, but also in the day-to-day aspects of life. How do you envision your daily routines, your interactions, your leisure time? What hobbies or interests do you want to pursue, both individually and together?

This process of alignment doesn't mean losing your individuality; rather, it's about harmonizing your personal goals with your shared objectives to create a melody that resonates with both of you.

A vital aspect of this vision is embracing each stage of your life together with grace and adaptability. Just as each season brings its own beauty and challenges, so do the different stages of your marriage.

Whether you're navigating the early days of marital bliss, the complexities of raising a family, or the quietude of later years, each phase offers unique opportunities for growth and deepening your bond.

Moreover, the vision for your future also encompasses a commitment to continual self-improvement and nurturing the marital bond. It's recognizing that as you each evolve and grow, so does your relationship.

This growth necessitates a commitment to ongoing communication, a willingness to adapt, and an openness to learning from each other. It's about-facing life's challenges together, turning obstacles into steppingstones for growth, and celebrating each victory as a testament to your strength as a couple.

As you journey through this chapter, remember that a vision for your marriage is more than a shared dream; it's a roadmap for your life together.

It's about setting intentions for how you want to grow, love, and live together. "The YOU Power in Your Marriage" is a guide to creating and nurturing this vision, a testament to the belief that with purpose, love, and mutual support, the journey of marriage can be the most fulfilling adventure of your life.

Envisioning a Lifetime of Growth and Love

Your vision for the future is a reflection of the hopes, dreams, and values you and your partner hold. It's about imagining not just the milestones you want to reach together but also the everyday moments that build the richness of your life as a couple. This vision encompasses the growth you both aspire to achieve – personally, professionally, spiritually, and as a unit.

1. **Dreaming Together**: Start by dreaming together. What does a fulfilling life look like for both of you? This could include aspirations like traveling the world, achieving career goals, nurturing a family, or contributing to your community. It's about aligning these dreams and turning them into a shared vision.

2. **Embracing Each Stage of Life**: Recognize that your marriage will evolve through different stages of life. Each stage brings its own challenges and joys. Embrace each of these stages with an open heart and a willingness to adapt and grow together.

3. **Nurturing a Lifelong Partnership**: Envisioning a future together means nurturing a relationship that goes beyond the surface. It's about building a partnership that is rooted in mutual respect, deep understanding, and an unwavering commitment to each other.

Continuing the Journey of Self-Improvement and Marital Fulfillment

A key part of your vision for the future involves the continuous journey of self-improvement and marital fulfillment. It's about recognizing that personal growth and the growth of your relationship are intertwined.

1. **Personal Development**: Commit to your personal growth and encourage your partner in their self-improvement journey. As individuals, your growth contributes to the strength and happiness of your marriage.

2. **Evolving Together**: As you both grow, ensure that your relationship evolves too. Keep the lines of communication open, continue to learn from each other, and make room for change and new experiences.

3. **Celebrating Milestones and Creating Memories**: Along your journey, celebrate the milestones you reach and cherish the memories you create. These are the markers of your shared journey, the moments that you'll look back on with joy and pride.

In this chapter, you'll explore how creating a shared vision for the future and committing to a lifelong journey of growth and love are essential to the longevity and fulfillment of your marriage. "The YOU Power in Your Marriage" is about understanding that a vision for the future is not just a dream to aspire to; it's a commitment to continuous growth, shared experiences, and unwavering love that makes every moment of your journey together worthwhile.

Conclusion

As we reach the concluding pages of "The YOU Power in Your Marriage," it's a moment to pause and reflect on the journey you have embarked upon. This book has not just been a collection of chapters; it has been a journey of discovery, learning, and growth. It's a journey that started with the individual – with you – and expanded to encompass the vast, intricate dynamics of marital life.

Reflecting on the Journey

Think back to where this journey began, to your understanding of yourself and your marriage before turning these pages. Reflect on the insights you've gained, the lessons learned, and the changes you've begun to implement. Each chapter was a step towards a deeper understanding of how the individual growth of each partner is intrinsically linked to the health and happiness of a marriage.

You've explored the importance of communication, the art of balancing individuality with togetherness, the transformative power of forgiveness, and the beauty of building a shared vision for the future. These are not just concepts; they are tools and insights that can guide you in nurturing a fulfilling and resilient marital relationship.

The Enduring Power of Self-Transformation in Marriage

As you move forward, carry with you the enduring truth that your personal growth and transformation have immense power in your marriage. The journey of self-improvement is continuous, and every step you take in becoming the best version of yourself adds to the strength and harmony of your union. Your willingness to grow, to embrace change, and to work towards a better you is a gift not just to yourself, but to your partner and your marriage.

Remember, the essence of "The YOU Power in Your Marriage" is the recognition that a strong, loving, and lasting marriage is built by two individuals who are committed to their own growth as well as the growth of their relationship. It's about finding the perfect balance where personal development and marital harmony coexist and enhance each other.

As you close this book, know that the journey doesn't end here. It continues in your everyday life, in your interactions with your partner, and in your commitment to nurture the love that binds you together. Let the principles and insights you've gained be your guides and let the power of your transformation illuminate your path in marriage.

Small Group Discussion Plan

Exploring 'The YOU Power in Your Marriage' with Scriptural Insights

Introduction: This series of discussions will delve into "The YOU Power in Your Marriage," integrating scriptural insights to deepen our understanding of personal growth and its impact on marital harmony.

Session 1: Understanding Self-Improvement in Marriage

- Discuss the importance of personal growth in a marriage. Reflect on Ephesians 4:15-16 about growing in every way more and more like Christ.

- Share how individual changes, guided by principles like those in Philippians 2:4, can positively impact the marital relationship.

Session 2: Communication as a Key to Connection

- Share personal experiences where effective communication, as advised in James 1:19, strengthened your relationship.

- Explore strategies for improving communication skills within your marriage, reflecting on Proverbs 18:21.

Session 3: Balancing Individuality and Togetherness

- Discuss challenges and benefits of maintaining individuality in marriage, considering Genesis 2:24's perspective on unity.

- Share how you and your partner support each other's growth, in line with 1 Corinthians 7:7's views on individual gifts.

Session 4: The Role of Forgiveness and Letting Go

- Discuss the process and importance of forgiveness in relationships, reflecting on Ephesians 4:32.

- Share experiences of forgiving or being forgiven, and its impact on your marriage, inspired by Matthew 18:21-22.

Session 5: Building and Sharing a Vision for the Future
- Talk about your shared dreams, in light of Proverbs 29:18, where having a vision is emphasized.

- Reflect on supporting each other in achieving aspirations, inspired by Ecclesiastes 4:9-10.

Session 6: The Power of Shared Experiences
- Share memorable experiences that strengthened your marital bond, in the spirit of Ecclesiastes 9:9.
- Discuss how creating new memories can fortify your marriage, considering Hebrews 10:24-25's call for encouragement.

Session 7: Navigating Challenges and Conflicts
- Explore how you handle conflicts and challenges, reflecting on James 3:17-18's wisdom for peace-making.

- Share strategies that have helped overcome difficult times, inspired by Romans 12:12.

Session 8: Continuing the Journey of Self-Improvement
- Reflect on ongoing personal and marital growth, in the context of Philippians 1:6.

- Discuss steps for continued growth, drawing inspiration from 2 Peter 3:18.

Conclusion: Conclude by summarizing key learnings from the book, integrating them with Biblical principles. Encourage each member to continue applying these insights in their marriages.

Appendices

Exercises and Activities for Couples

The journey of marriage is both rewarding and challenging, and it often helps to have practical tools to enhance and deepen your connection. In these appendices, you will find a variety of exercises and activities specifically designed for couples. These are intended to strengthen your bond, improve communication, and encourage growth and understanding in your relationship.

1. **Weekly Check-In Exercise**: Set aside time each week to check in with each other. During this time, share your feelings, discuss any concerns, and express appreciation for each other. This exercise fosters open communication and ensures that both partners feel heard and valued.

2. **Date Night Ideas Jar**: Create a jar filled with date night ideas. Each week, take turns drawing an idea from the jar. This activity adds spontaneity and excitement to your relationship, ensuring that you regularly spend quality time together.

3. **Gratitude Journaling Together**: Start a gratitude journal where you both write down things you are grateful for in your

marriage. This can be daily affirmations, appreciation for each other, or joyful moments you've shared. Regularly review this journal together to remind yourselves of the positive aspects of your relationship.

4. **Communication Role-Play**: Engage in role-play exercises where you act out various scenarios. This can include practicing active listening, expressing difficult emotions, or working through a hypothetical conflict. This activity enhances understanding and empathy between partners.

5. **Vision Board Creation**: Collaboratively create a vision board that represents your shared dreams and goals. This visual representation can include images, quotes, or symbols that reflect your aspirations as a couple. Revisit and update it annually to keep your shared vision alive and relevant.

6. **Love Letters Exchange**: Write love letters to each other, expressing your feelings, hopes, and commitments. Set a time to exchange and read these letters. This activity allows for deep emotional expression and strengthens the romantic aspect of your relationship.

7. **Couples' Reflection Retreat**: Plan an annual retreat where you spend time away from daily routines to reflect on your relationship. Use this time to discuss your growth as a couple, address any challenges, and plan for the future.

8. **Shared Hobby or Class**: Take up a new hobby or enroll in a class together. This could be anything from cooking classes, dance

lessons, to a book club. Shared hobbies provide opportunities to bond, learn together, and create new, fun memories.

These exercises and activities are designed to be flexible and adaptable to your unique relationship dynamics. They serve as tools to help you both grow closer, understand each other better, and keep the spark of your marriage alive. Remember, the most important aspect is the commitment to engage in these activities together, nurturing the bond that you share.

Sade's Story: A Journey of Self-Discovery and Transformation

Sade's story is one of realization, responsibility, and resilience. Married for eight years to her college sweetheart, Sade's marriage was a source of joy and companionship.

However, over the years, Sade noticed a growing distance between her and her husband. Conversations became brief, date nights rare, and the spark that once illuminated their relationship seemed to dim.

During a heart-to-heart conversation, her husband gently expressed his concerns about their fading connection. He missed the adventurous, energetic woman he fell in love with, someone who was passionate about life and took care of herself, both emotionally and physically. It was a difficult conversation, but it opened Sade's eyes to a truth she had been avoiding she had stopped prioritizing her well-being and, in turn, their relationship.

One aspect that particularly stood out was her uncontrolled weight gain over the years. Sade realized that it wasn't just about the physical appearance but what it represented. The weight gain was a symptom of neglecting her own health and well-being, of putting her needs last, and losing a part of her vibrant self in the daily grind of life.

Determined to bring about a change, Sade embarked on a journey of self-improvement. It wasn't just about losing weight; it was about regaining her health, her confidence, and reigniting her zest for life. She started with small, sustainable changes to her diet, incorporating more wholesome foods and mindful eating practices. She rediscovered her love for physical activities, starting with brisk walks, then gradually moving to more structured workouts.

As the weeks turned into months, the changes became evident. Sade was not only shedding the extra weight but was also glowing with a newfound vitality.

Her transformation went beyond the physical. She became more energetic, more engaged in her life and relationship. Her husband noticed these changes too, not just in her appearance but in her renewed spirit, her happiness, and her confidence.

Their relationship blossomed anew. They started enjoying outdoor activities together, rediscovering the joys of their early years of marriage. Their conversations grew deeper, their bond stronger, and the love that had seemed distant now flowed freely and warmly between them.

Sade's journey was a testament to the power of personal responsibility and transformation. Her intentional efforts to improve her physical health had a profound effect on her emotional and relationship health. She had not only saved her marriage but had also rediscovered herself.

Sade's story is a powerful reminder that sometimes, the path to healing a relationship starts with healing and transforming oneself.

Made in the USA
Columbia, SC
14 October 2024